INSIDE the ROPES

DEE DARDEN

**Life on the LPGA Tour
as Seen Through the Lens
of Photographer and Caddy
DEE DARDEN**

**Foreword by
NANCY LOPEZ**

CONCEPT AND DESIGN BY BILL SPENCER

INSIDE THE ROPES
Photographed and written by Dee Darden
Conceived and designed by Bill Spencer
Foreword by Nancy Lopez

Library of Congress Catalog Number 93-073239
ISBN 0-9637780-0-5
Printed in Hong Kong by Imago Sales, U.S.A.

Special thanks to Charles Mechem, Commissioner of the LPGA,
and to Lee Robbins, President of the Tournament Sponsors
Association, and its members, without whose support and
assistance this book would not have been possible. We
sincerely thank you all.

All photographs by Dee Darden except as individually credited.

Edited by A.E. Thompson

Cover photograph by Chris Hoeler of Christopher Richards, Inc.
Computer graphics for cover provided by Ken Sagnelli and
Tim Smith, Planetwide Productions, Stamford, CT.

Published by:
Fairway Publications
c/o Riber Sports Marketing, Inc.
7442 Jager Court
Cincinnati, Ohio 45230
Tel.: 513-624-2100
Fax: 513-624-2110

Dedication

This book is dedicated to my wife, Jeannie, and to Bill's wife, Denise. If patience were dollar bills, they could solve the national debt. And to Bill's sons Nathaniel and Benjamin. Thank you all. You're the greatest.

Foreword
BY
NANCY LOPEZ

For 5 years Dee Darden was with me every step of the way on the golf course. He was my caddy and my best friend "Inside The Ropes." I felt totally confident with him by my side. We won 11 tournaments together. His perception, course management, and meticulous ways always made me play better. Dee saw things that others missed, whether it be a wind change, grain on the greens, or hardness of fairways, he had already thought it through, computed it, and had the answer ready.

"Inside The Ropes" is a great personal testament to his uncanny ability as a photographer to capture special moments on our tour, preserving them forever like no one else has. The book is a picture story about our tours great expressions, our joys, our happiness, and many of the funny events that only someone who understands the game so well can do. You will see family . . . friends . . . competitors . . . mothers . . . ladies. It is a story told through a masters eye with insight and perception. Dee portrays the LPGA tour as a family, not just fierce competitors. There is so much more to golf than just teeing it up, playing the courses, going home, going to sleep, then waking to practice. Dee and his partner Bill Spencer not only attempt to show the complete picture, they succeed beyond reproach.

You will get to know the players a little better, by putting their faces with their names. You will see our international players, Patty Sheehan's picture perfect swing, the look of determination on Pat Bradley's face, Betsy King's strive for perfection, Amy Alcott's relentless pursuit of the Hall of Fame, and Meg Mallon's million dollar smile.

"Inside The Ropes" certainly has captured the physical me. My golf swing, my family, my personality, desires and emotions are all on display. Great going Bill and Dee. It's a work that's long over due, but well worth the wait.

I will treasure my copy and it will be displayed proudly in my home for all to see.

Your friend & former employer,
Love, Nancy

Letter From Commissioner Mechem

The Ladies' Professional Golf Association has enjoyed tremendous growth, and success over the last few years. Much of that success is due to the wide variety of personalities that make up the tour. What photographer and former caddy, Dee Darden, and designer Bill Spencer have done so well, is capture the warmth, humor and professionalism of the players on photographs that literally bounce off the pages.

Whether you know anything about the LPGA Tour prior to scanning this book, you are certain to take away a good feeling and have a better understanding about tour life "Inside the Ropes." If you are already familiar with the tour and some of it's many personalities, then this book will make you smile, as you turn from page to page and encounter yet another "sneak peek" into life on the LPGA Tour.

We hope you enjoy this pictorial journey through the greatest professional women's sports organization in the world, The LPGA Tour!

Sincerely,

Charles S. Mechem, Jr.
Commissioner
Ladies Professional Golf Association

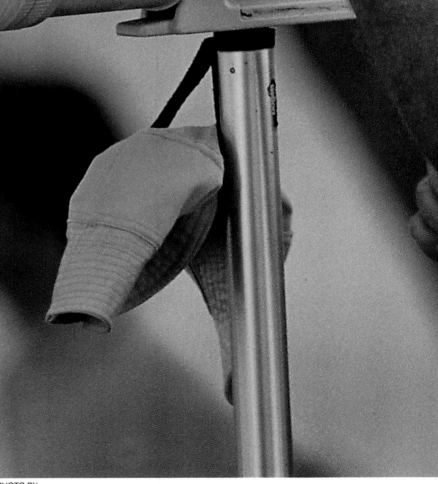

My son, Curt, lives in L.A., and he came to visit me at the Nabisco Dinah Shore in 1992. I immediately put him to work lugging one of my cameras. He took this shot of me turning fun into finances.

Hardly working at the Dinah.

8

When Bill Spencer, the art director for Golf World Magazine and I started this book, we had no preconceived ideas about format or content. I am pleased that this sequence on Beth turned out to be the opening pages of "Inside The Ropes." She is a rare talent, and I'm glad to call her my friend.

10

*Often the fans and media see Beth Daniel as a club-slamming, fiery, fairway warrior.
I see Beth as the caring person sharing her first major tournament victory
with her brother, Tony, niece, Jordan, and nephew, Rob.
This will probably end our friendship!*

*I*f you like color, booming drives, exciting golf and beautiful scenery, join the McGann Fan Club.
Michelle has already changed the look and length of women's golf, and just barely in her 20's. Good grief!

Dale Eggeling coming out of the sand on No. 17 at the Dinah. Dale plays horses – literally. She owns several.

Cathy Johnston joined a small group of players whose first victory was a "major" when she won the 1990 du Maurier Ltd. Classic.

Jane Geddes and Jessy Harris. What a pair – firing and hiring and firing their way across country. When they get their teamwork going, they win.

13

*T*ammie Green and John Schiffer are being carted back to the 18th tee by tour official John Lillvis for a play-off with JoAnne Carner. Tammie won the '93 HealthSouth Palm Beach Classic with a 30 foot putt on the first extra hole.

*D*onna Earley, who caddies for Amy Benz, is constantly being teased about her long legs. They're not that long, Donna!

*K*aren Davies at the office.

*C*aroline Keggi's caddy, Bruce Lamdin, will be a familiar face to many fans. From the late '70s through the mid '80s he was a full time caddy for Hollis Stacy and later Jan Stephenson. He has resumed active law practice but still comes out on occasion to bag for Keggi. Once you've been "Inside The Ropes" and have made the victory walk up 18 fairway, ordinary life is pretty dull.

*D*uring the first week in December, the JCPenney Mixed Team Classic is held in Florida. Often a player will ask a friend to carry her bag if her regular caddy isn't available. Judy Dickinson asked her friend, Doreen LaDonna, to loop the load.

*R*obin Walton is looking for the green.

*S*ue Smith takes a tea break.

*S*helley Hamlin is enjoying her first victory after returning to the tour following recovery from breast cancer. She beat everybody again at the ShopRite Classic in '93.

Guess who got married?
Heather Farr and Gorän Lingmerth tied the knot and cut the cake March 20, 1993, in Phoenix.

Ayako Okamoto is one very talented woman. All the great players I know have a "feel" for victory. They sense when it's probable. Ayako has that greatness.

Gardner and Judy Dickinson checking one of her clubs. Gardner's no voodoo guru! He knows what he's talking about.

*T*his photo summarizes why I love this game so much. Tina Barrett's Mixed Team partner, Fred Funk, and his caddy are seriously pointing out the pitfalls of break, speed, grain, etc. She made the putt anyway. Her eyes said she would. In golf – it is you who do!

*A*my Alcott can entomb herself in deep concentration for extended periods of time.

*S*he occasionally escapes.

*J*udy and Gardner Dickinson's back-to-back wins – Chip and Putt – alias Barron and Spencer. Three term president of the LPGA and winner of the 1992 Patty Berg Award. Most respected and admired. Beautiful swing and talented player. Did I leave anything out?

John and Frank are two of the greatest marshals anywhere. They've been with the McDonald's tournament since day one. They make my birthday special every year.

Jenny Lidback maintains citizenship in both Peru and Sweden, She's a quiet, intelligent, multi-lingual, friendly person.

*O*ne of the truly classic and beautiful finishing holes on the LPGA Tour. No. 17 at Mission Hills. Very demanding par 3.

*M*eg Mallon passes the jacket to Betsy King at the '92 Mazda Championship in Bethesda, Md.

24

Laura Davies – England's finest and a class lady. Just starting to play in my opinion.

Sandra Palmer – what a charmer – just keeps rolling along – stays in great shape, and I hope to see her for many more years.

*D*ave Kebely and his wife, Linda, own and manage a day care center in Seattle. Dave loves to caddy and often will pop up on Lauren Howe's bag.

*M*eg Mallon testing the wind – It's blowing straight down, Meg!

*"B*ig Vic" Fergon has had a very successful career with two victories and $1,000,000 in earnings. I watched her win her first tournament in 1979 at the Lady Stroh's in Dearborn, Michigan.

*P*am Wright and her caddy, Suzette Combs, four-eyeing a birdie putt. Good one-eyed photo, Dee!

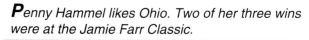

*M*y wife, Jeannie, worked for Lauren Howe in the early '80s. They won the 1983 Mayflower in Indianapolis. Lauren came on tour in the late '70s. I thought she was the most beautiful woman I had ever seen – still do!

Doug and Dottie Mochrie. Dottie gives Doug a lot of credit for her tournament success. I think she's absolutely right!

Light your fire, Amy. Kick some rear, Dear – like you did mine and Beth's in '83 at the Dinah. Nobody would mind if you did it again.

Party time at the Chocolate Town Open. This was a two club, par three, beer and cheer, nine-hole event. A nice mid-year break. Shown are Linda Hunt, Sue Witters, Kathryn Young, and Margaret Ward.

*N*o one has ever played the game better than Pat Bradley did in 1986. She won three major tournaments: The Nabisco Dinah Shore, the LPGA Championship, the du Maurier Ltd. Classic and finished fifth in the U.S Women's Open.

In my opinion, she has one of the best short games in golf and is the best long putter in history.

*T*he finishing hole at Innisbrook Resort in Tarpon Springs is most pleasing to the eye. I have tried every year to capture the shadow patterns, sand and light. I think I got it.

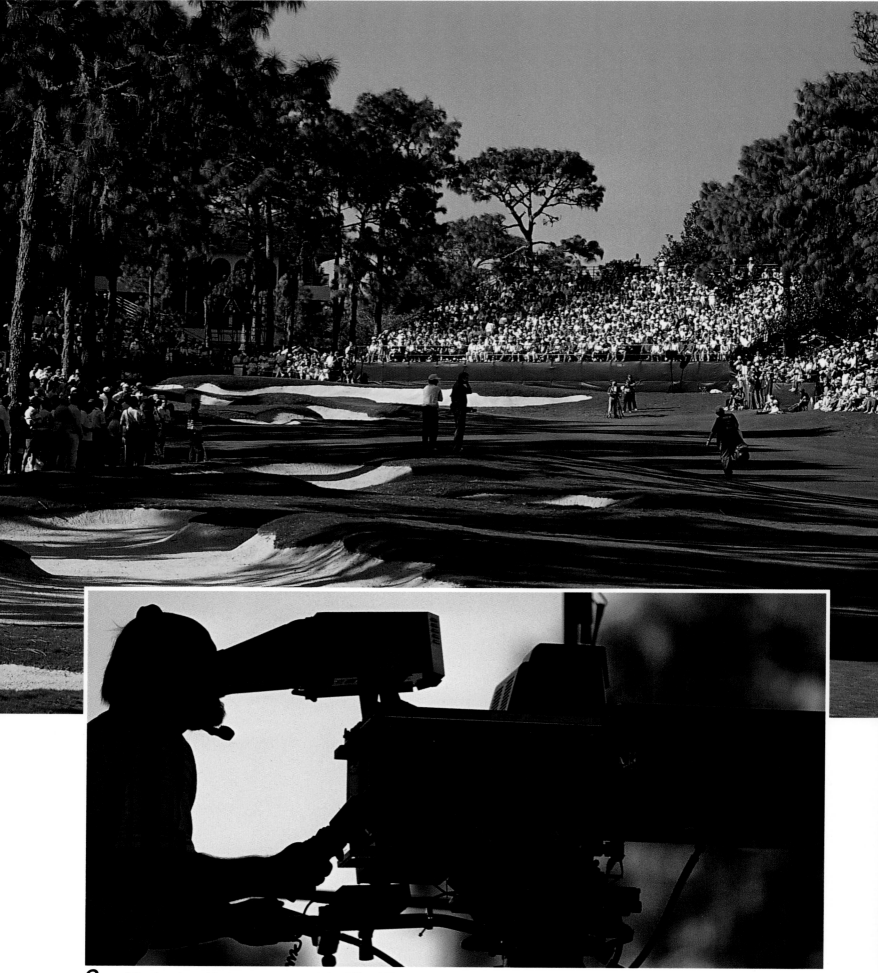

*O*ne of the hard working cameramen at the Mixed Team event.

*D*eborah McHaffie and her nephew Evan were taking a little break to enjoy the Las Vegas weather and scenery.

*W*hat's that fellow doing on the green? Why, he's painting the hole white so it will be more visible to the TV viewing audience! And you thought the media didn't care.

33

A hale and hearty, healthy and happy Suzanne Jackson before cancer struck. She's recovering nicely and by her own admission "feeling fine."

*C*athy Reynolds was playing a practice round at the Desert Inn in Las Vegas.

*L*ynn Adams is a good friend. When I'm not at the tournament site, I always check the sports page for her score.

Deb Richard hitting a very fine fairway bunker shot at the '92 U.S. Women's Open. Every golfer could use some of her intensity and concentration.

Susie Berning was playing in the Ping tournament in Phoenix in '92. Her daughter, Robin was giving her a playing lesson walking down No.15 fairway. Susie has won three U.S. Women's Opens. Only Mickey Wright, Betsy Rawls, and Hollis Stacy can claim that.

Laurie Rinker-Graham and her hub, Rob, at the JCPenney Classic. Rob sometimes gets talked into the caddy mode.

*K*athy Baker Guadagnino and her husband/caddy, Joe, were trying to figure a way out of the mess Kathy got herself in on No. 9 at Crooked Stick. Kathy's first victory was the U.S. Women's Open at Baltusrol in 1985.

*D*ale Eggeling, hampered by a bad knee, lining up a putt.

*Y*es, Dina Ammaccapane is Danielle's sister. She's a good player, and she also plays very fast. It is not unusual to see her ball in flight while her playing partner's ball is still airborne. She and Garbacz could probably play nine holes in an hour.

*B*eth Daniel holding court on the driving range. It's one of her favorite activities!

*C*olleen Walker has been one of the most consistent players since the late '80s.

*M*eg Mallon and Dana Lofland-Dormann take a moment to say "Hi" during the '92 Mixed Team at Innisbrook.

Heather Farr at the Sara Lee Classic. I've known her since she was sixteen. We went through pro school together in 1985. Her long and courageous fight with cancer started in the late '80s and ended November 20, 1993. Sadly we lost Heather, but her spirit still lives in her quest to conquer the mountain.

Laura Baugh was seven months pregnant at the Phar-Mor Classic in Inverrary in 1990. She shot 67 on Friday to make the cut. "The ball goes farther with two people swinging at it," she said.

Kris Tschetter looking good on No. 6 tee in Nashville. Her game has improved dramatically in the '90s.

39

No photo has ever pleased me more than this one. The eighth tee in Tallahassee was backed up.
I was pot-shotting people – so-so stuff – mostly boring. Then they saw me.
ACTION – CAMERA – GIVE ME SOMETHING!

*T*hree super stars saved a ho-hum day. Sometimes you hope lucky – sometimes you get! L-R Juli Inkster – Patty Sheehan – Nancy Lopez.

Nancy's regular caddy, Tommy Thorpe, hurt his back and Nancy's husband, Ray Knight, picked up the bag. Ray's getting to be a good pinch hitting caddy.

Hiromi Kobayashi getting her mind set on the par-3 17th at the McDonald's.

Martha Nause in Vegas working on a repeating stroke. You can get the same rhythm on the slot machine, Martha!

*J*o Ann Washam is retired now but she was a tough competitor and had several wins. I saw her recently in Florida and she looked like she always did – about 15.

*K*ris Tschetter had her first win with Mixed Team partner, Billy Andrade during the JCPenney Classic at Innisbrook in '91.
The Mixed Team is a good "first-win" tournament.

*D*oug Mochrie catches his victorious wife, Dottie, moments after the winning putt fell at the Dinah in '92. First "major" crowns are very special.

*J*uli Inkster and Dottie Mochrie leave the 18th green at the Nabisco Dinah Shore all tied in '92. Dottie won on the first playoff hole.

After Patty Sheehan won the '93 Mazda Championship, accepted the trophy and the check, held the formal press conference, and had her sweet taste of victory— things got a little crazy! She took a dive, knickers and all.

***P**atty joined a soggy Mazda crew including Meg Mallon, Beth Daniel, Jan Thompson, and a flamingo. "Bottom", formed a dance trio with Beth & Jan— and in general celebrated in typical Sheehan style. This was Mazda's swan song. They will be missed.*

During the post victory ceremony prominent people say and do important things. No one is more prominent than Jan Thompson from Mazda Motor. She is a gracious lady and the driving force behind the very successful Mazda LPGA Championship. Jan, Betsy King, and Roger Malbie are summarizing events on the NBC telecast.

PHOTO BY JEANNIE

Jane Crafter and Donna White enjoying watermelon on the Mall in Washington, D.C. Sometimes all play and no work is more fun than chasing birdies.

48

*L*auri Merten is a consistent player, very warm and personable. My wife, Jeannie, caddied for her many times on a fill-in basis and always spoke highly of her. I like players who are unaffected and friendly. Lauri fits that description perfectly.

*H*ow many people in life can go by one word and be instantly recognized? In golf, "Nancy" is enough. I caddied for her from 1984 through 1988. She can play. She never quits. She's nicer than everybody thinks.

*S*he's also more deadly than a Ping putter. But, when she enters her home, golf gives way to family and motherhood. Am I a fan? Just her best.

Liselotte Neumann established her star credentials as winner of the 1988 U.S. Women's Open at Five Farms in Baltimore, Md. Recently, her talents emerged again as a winning member of the 1992 European Solheim Cup Team.

Lotta and her caddy, Mark Scott, discussing yardage on the 17th tee in Nashville.

Lotta was waiting to hit at the sixth hole at the Dinah. A Japanese photographer and friend of mine, Kaz, was shooting her also. "For a calendar," he said, "and what about you, Dee-san?" "Pure enjoyment," I said.

*J*ane Geddes and Bobby Inman *no longer work together as a player/caddy team.*
But they're still friends. Jane recently bought this photo and has it in her home.

*L*ife can go by pretty fast, but with a good lens you can stop a piece of it. Like this frame of Amy Benz.

*F*rom '89 through '92 Judy Dickinson served three terms as president of the LPGA, had twin boys, Barron and Spencer, played in 88 tournaments, and made over $700,000. Whew!

*W*hen Lenore Rittenhouse found out that she could carry her own golf bag in the U.S. Women's Open in '93, she did. "It wasn't meant to attract attention," she said. "I thought it would be fun, and it was!"

55

Patty Sheehan and JoAnne Dost, a former player, enjoying Patty's post U.S. Women's Open victory party in Oakmont, Pa. JoAnne has her own photography business.

Kelly Robbins had a fine first year earning nearly $100,000 and finishing third in the '92 rookie race. Her first professional victory came in May '93 at Corning, N.Y. According to her caddy, Tim Atsedes, she hits it big and has a great attitude.

Sue Thomas, working hard, learning the game.

Jeannie and I put more than 200,000 miles on this Holiday Rambler from 1982 through 1989. One of the pluses about RV life – you're always home – even if you break down.

Kathy Postlewait and Debbie Raso take a small nutrition break.

Tracy Kerdyk has a penchant for holes-in-one.
She's had four.

Alice Ritzman. A proud Ping player.

These fans obviously support the Centel Classic. I buy that. Friendly signs are rare these days.

Tina Barrett converting energy to cash.

Michelle Estill and I were both behind a tree.
My shot came out better.

*W*hen you get to photograph players like Cindy Figg-Currier, how can you not become a fan?

*N*eil Armstrong, Marilyn and Charlie Mechem, sharing a moment at the second annual Capitol Hill visit. Neil is a member of the LPGA Commissioner's Advisory Council and the first man to walk on the moon.

*Oh, to win the OPEN – to hug the trophy – to prance the dance – to savor champagne from the depths –
to know the glow and warmth of athletic victory so rare and so very special. You are a most favored and fortunate
person, Patty Sheehan – but I think you know that.*

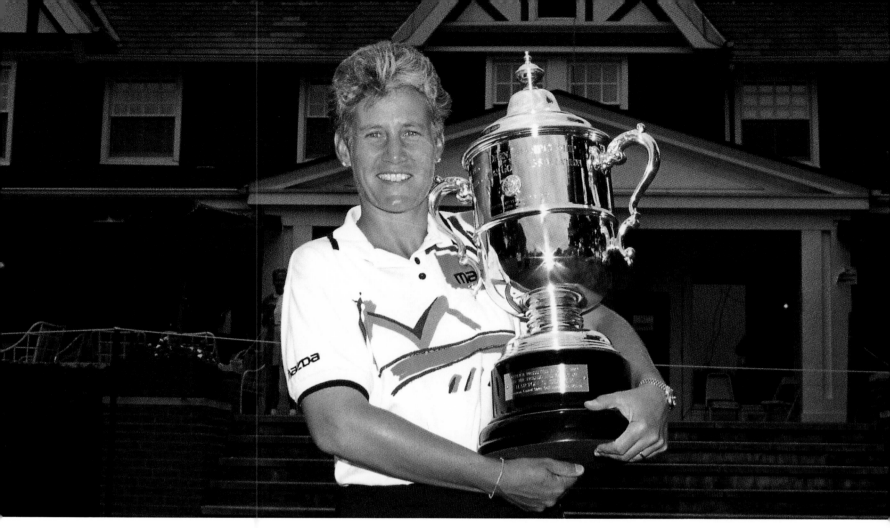

At Oakmont, Pa., in July '92, Patty finally got her Open victory. She birdied Nos. 17 and 18 to force a play-off with Inkster. Then on Monday she would not be beat. You're a Pistol, Patty!

61

*D*ana Lofland sifting silver dollars at the Desert Inn following her victory in 1992.

Suzanne Jackson, Director of Tournament Operations, is winning the fight against breast cancer. The LPGA Association is providing some very strong support to help the players.

Kris Tschetter and her caddy, Eddie Pelz, were sharing a funny story on the driving range. This is what I enjoy so much about the LPGA. There seems to be time for these moments.

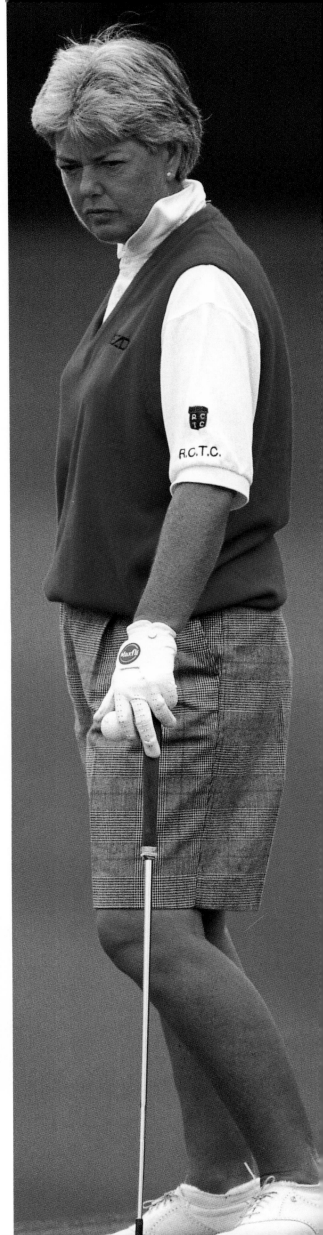

*P*at Bradley studying the putting terrain at Inverrary in '92. Her stalking look has been a trademark over the years.

*H*eather Drew and caddy, Donald Sneedon Jr., enjoying a nice finish at the Ping/Welch's Championship in Tucson.

*S*ally Little has long held the reputation as a premier sand player. This shot doesn't hurt her image.

Susan Sanders is a friend of mine. I made a personal photo album of her one year in San Jose, Calif.– met her family – nice people.

Marianne Morris is off to her best start in '93. Some people just never give up!

Barb Bunkowsky practicing chip shots at the '92 Mazda Championship.

66

*A*lcott and Inkster share a caring moment on the putting green at the McDonald's in '92. Many of the players grew up together with junior golf, then college and later the pros. When emotional events, good and bad, occur, there is a lot of immediate support.

*T*ina Barrett on the range in Phoenix, pounding her Pings.

*G*ail Graham – good profile.

*A*yako Okamoto and John Killeen were on No. 9 at the Nabisco when they saw the "Big Eye" tracking them.

*A*llison Finney – get that putter going, girl!

*M*artha Faulconer. I like her game and her attitude. Hang tough, Martha!

*T*here is no way
to take a bad shot
of Liselotte Neumann.
They start at magnificent
and work upward.

69

I was standing beside Betsy on top of the hill at the last hole Sunday in Bethesda, Md. She was 16 under par, lying 20 feet from the hole, with a 10 shot lead. Another MAJOR, one more– yawn— win. When suddenly, MISS PRISTINE herself started fleet footing down the right ropes, palm slapping everybody with a hand. I was so surprised I nearly missed the shot. What a day–17 May '92.

MAZDA LPGA CHAMPIONSHIP

PLAYER	HOLE	1	2	3	4	5	6	7	8	9	10	11	12	13	14	15	16	17	18
START	PAR	4	5	4	3	4	4	4	3	4	4	5	3	5	4	4	3	4	4
12 KING		12	13	14	14	14	15	15	15	15	15	15	16	16	16	16	16	16	17
7 ALFREDSSON		6	6	6	7	7	6	5	5	5	6	6	5		3	3	2	2	3
6 INKSTER		6	6	6	6	6	6	6	5	5	5	6	6	7	7	6	6	6	
6 CARNER		6	6	6	6	6	6	5	5	5	5	6	6	5	7	7	7	6	6
4 NEUMANN		3	3	3	3	3	4	4	4	5	5	5	5	5	6	6	4		
3 SHEEHAN		3	3	3	4	4	4	3	3	3	4	4	5	5	5	4	4		
3 RITZMAN		3	3	2	2	2	3	3	3	4	4	4	5	6	6	6	6		
0 NOBLE		0	0	0	1	1	1	2	3	3	4	4	5	3	3	3	2	2	

If you have ever played the Bethesda C.C. in Maryland, and had not watched the tournament, you may think the score board is a fake. Folks – it happened – I saw it!

*T*his is a typical Betsy King finish. She doesn't particularly like it , but she doesn't like it when she changes either. Wish I had it. I could use $4,000,000.

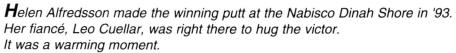

Helen Alfredsson made the winning putt at the Nabisco Dinah Shore in '93. Her fiancé, Leo Cuellar, was right there to hug the victor. It was a warming moment.

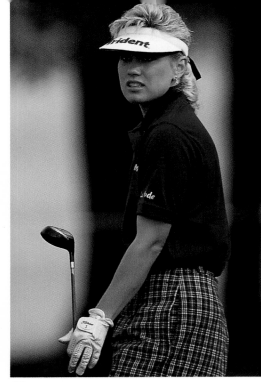

Kate Hughes had a good year in '92 .

Sherri Steinhauer came on tour in the mid '80s. She didn't have much game in her then. Boy, has that changed.

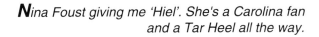

Nina Foust giving me 'Hiel'. She's a Carolina fan and a Tar Heel all the way.

*B*ig Momma, JoAnne Carner, defies gravity with this follow-through on No. 18 tee at the '92 Mazda Championship. *If you've never seen her play, maybe you should re-evaluate your priorities.*

In the early '80s, if you wanted to win, you probably had to beat Donna Caponi. She was very tough. We called her "The General" because she directed everything: players – fans – caddies. Now she's directing her energies and experiences to telecasting. Good luck to you, Donna. You are missed.

Pearl

Donna

Pearl Sinn, Liselotte Neumann, Donna Andrews, and Val Skinner represent the modern LPGA very well. They are hard working, personable, dedicated players.

Lotta

Val

Lisa Walters had her best year in '92 with over $100,000 and one win. The brace she is wearing helped her heal from reconstructive surgery in '91. Lisa captured her second tournament victory by defending her title at the ITOKI Hawaiian Ladies Open in '93.

*H*iromi Kobayashi is having her best year. She seems more comfortable and relaxed. She won the JAL Big Apple Classic in '93.

*T*his looks like Daytona Beach sand, but Muffin Spencer-Devlin was actually on the second hole at McDonald's.

*B*arbra Mizrahie and her son, Marc, were at the Phar-Mor tourney in Inverrary enjoying the event. Barbra is a former tour player and is a native of Surabaya, Indonesia.

*R*ick and Cindy Rarick are into their tenth year as a married caddy/player team. Many have tried, not many have survived. They're doing something right.

*J*udy Rankin won 26 tournaments in 11 years, from 1968 through 1979. Fans still see her often as an on-course color commentator for ESPN and other networks.

*I*n the late '80s, Nike provided shoes, raingear, jackets, shirts, etc. to about twenty full-time tour caddies. You will notice my wife, Jeannie, is wearing Reeboks. Ten percent never get the word!

Brandie Burton was studying her yardage book notes Sunday at the McDonald's in '92.
Sometimes you need a little break to rest your mind from tournament pressure.

*R*ay Knight filled in for me at the Mazda Stonebridge tourney in 1989. I was hobbling around the course with a lens and caught him on the 15th green. Ray's such a nice guy. But he's a better behind-the-ropes booster. It gets "cold" sometimes "Inside The Ropes."

*R*osie Jones was doing an interview via international satellite hook-up at the JAL Big Apple Classic in New Rochelle, N.Y.

*D*ottie Mochrie hit it big in 1992. She won Rolex Player of the Year and the Vare Trophy for low scoring average.

Dottie is a big force on tour now and could very well dominate in the next few years.

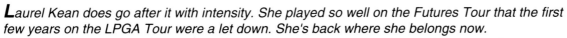

*M*arlene Hagge: LPGA charter member, trend setter.

*L*ynn Adams' birdie on No. 10 in Palm Springs.

*T*he Centel Tournament Director Lon Fellenz and Tour Official Barb Trammell were minding their own business when I passed by with a camera. Why don't you pretend you like each other, I said!

*M*arta Figueras-Dotti has a quiet golf swing, much like the Lopez tempo. Give it a try.

Danielle Ammaccapane played magnificent golf in the '90s. She hurt herself riding her horse in early '93 and is just now getting her game back. She's a top-10 player. You can count on her return.

*J*ane Crafter and Tommy Frank (alias "Motion") sharing a pleasant moment during a lull in play. Jane has a longer shaft in her driver. The extra length off the tee plays right into her excellent short game.

*T*he Whit — "I don't know why they let me keep my card!" An original. According to Betsy Rawls, Kathy Whitworth and Mickey Wright would win every other week, it seemed.

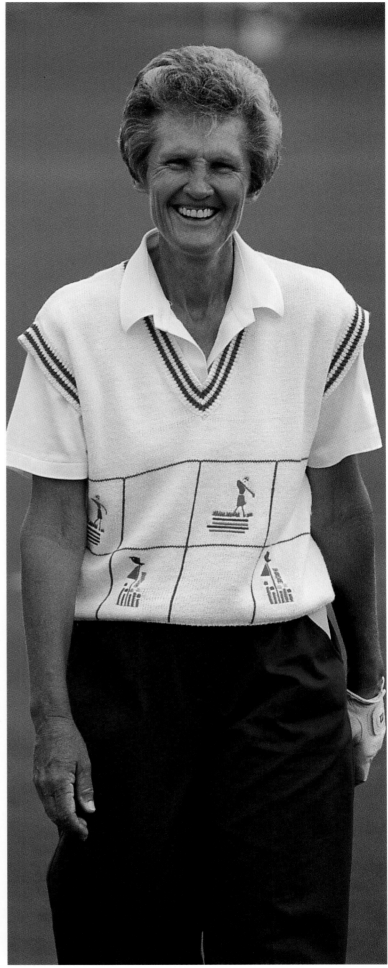

*O*k-Hee Ku is from Seoul, Korea. She came on tour in 1986. I watched her win her first tournament, the Standard Register Turquoise Classic in 1988.

I had the great fortune to caddy for her in Sleepy Hole in 1986. We finished fifth. I enjoyed every minute.

D*awn Coe-Jones at address position. She has really played good golf the last few years.
I can see nothing that will keep her from winning many events.*

The hat adds the color and charm, but her golf game is more fun to watch. Michelle McGann, a tower of power. Watch her progress, folks — she's gonna kill'em.

Harpo shows up all over the West Coast. He is a permanent fixture at the Nabisco Dinah Shore tourney. I met him in the early '80s. Harpo, my buddy Rick Aune and I, would pig out on Mexican food at the drop of a sombrero.

Barb Mucha has attacked the '90s with two wins and more than $350,000. Pretty fair golf!

*M*ust be McGann's hat fan club.

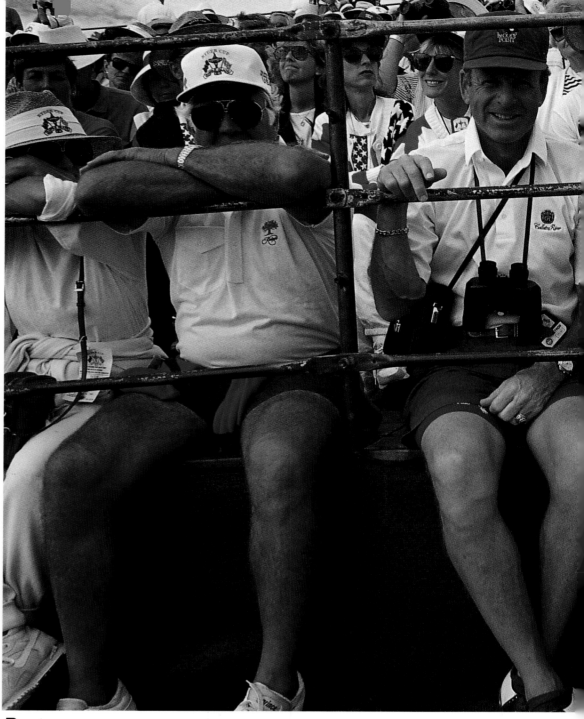

*R*uthie and Larry Harrison, Directors of the Shop Rite Classic, were enjoying the Ryder Cup on Kiawah Island, S. C.

*F*ans love to have their picture taken. Maybe they think they will turn up in some book!

*L*ook at Jane Geddes finish.
Perfect balance. Strong player.

Nancy's famous grin.

Meg Mallon giving a high-10 to a friend at the Mazda Championship.

Betsy Rawls getting a good drive at the Sprint Senior Challenge. Keep it in the air, Betsy. All the trouble's on the ground!

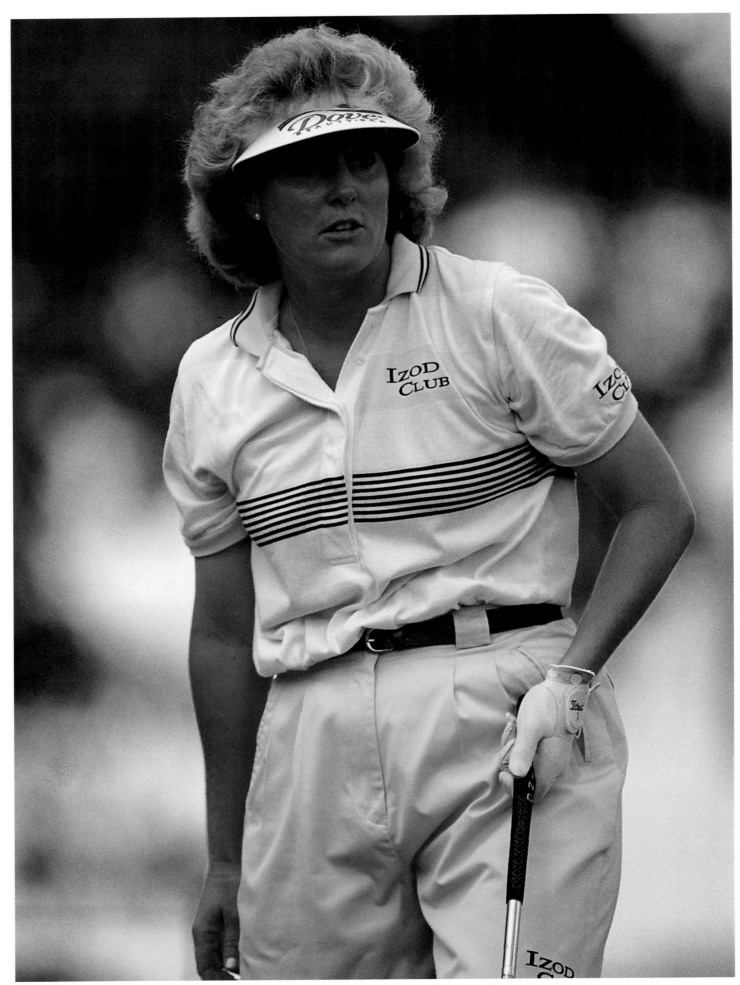

*B*etsy King struggled early in her career; Nancy has not known a similar struggle.

*B*etsy keeps getting better; Nancy is in the Hall of Fame. Two world class competitors. Stay tuned.

*M*y wife, Jeannie, caddied for Barb Bunkowsky in 1982. We've followed her career since then.

*L*aura Baugh was playing the 10th hole at McDonald's. I asked Bobby Cole, her husband, if I could get a shot of them on the 11th tee. After Laura hit her tee ball, she tore off to the porta potty. When she came out the other players were way down the fairway. I signaled them to go on, but they insisted. This is the shot I got – I've never thanked them properly until now.

*J*ulie Larsen working at her game and for the game.

*L*aura Bennett, Marketing and Promotions Director for Mazda Motor of America.

Robin Hood

Donna White

Laura Baugh

Liselotte Neumann

Jan Stephenson

94

Patty Sheehan

Maggie Will

What if a putt were as easy as a seven-footer making a slam dunk? A hole the size of a basket? Piece of cake from 30 feet.

Nanci Bowen

Juli Inkster

Beth Daniel

The "Tour Moms" photo was set-up for the local Boca Raton, Fla., media. I couldn't believe the patience of the mothers or the kids. Judy held those twins for an hour. She's the strongest woman in the world!

My wife had just given Nancy a present at her baby shower — a pair of baby Nike shoes: one blue and one pink.

*J*udy Dickinson, Myra Blackwelder, Barbara Mizrahie, Cathy Marino, Carol French, Terry-Jo Myers, Cathy Gerring and Laura Baugh.

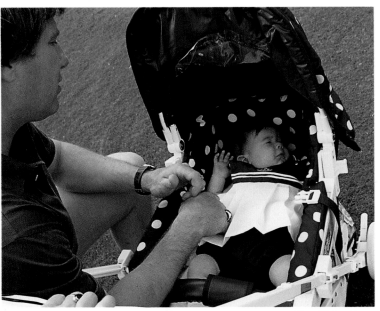

*R*ay Knight with baby, Torri Heather.

*J*uli Inkster and Hayley.

97

*K*ay Cockerill was the 1986 and '87 U.S. Women's Amateur champion. Her professional career is progressing nicely. I like to photograph her because she's so natural and unaffected. She glides down the fairway. Fun to watch.

*H*iromi Kobayashi has a nice smile to go with her game.
I don't know her very well; I'll have to work on that.

*W*hen I take Sherri Steinhauer's photograph,
I can't wait to get the slide back.

*K*atie Peterson-Parker is a two time all American and a former Curtis Cup member.

The legendary Mickey Wright. She makes it look so easy and so natural. I have admired many players, but Mickey is the only one for whom the phrase "In Awe Of" fits.

*K*athy Whitworth — golf's all time leading tournament winner with 88 victories. Mickey Wright is close with 82 victories. Their combined wins are 170. That's five full years of scheduled events.

*T*hese ten professionals, plus Mickey and Kathy, competed in the third annual Sprint Senior Challenge. From left they are Sandra Palmer, Marlene Hagge, Susie Berning, Donna Caponi, Louise Suggs, Carol Mann, Marilynn Smith, Betsy Rawls, Jane Blalock and Sandra Haynie.

When Mickey and Kathy finished their round in Tallahassee and performed their mutual admiration hug, I was there waiting. I will always cherish this photograph for who they are, and how it came to be.

When Mickey Wright finished her first round, several players lined up to get her autograph. Loretta Alderete, Michelle Estill, Nancy Harvey and Mary Murphy were just barely in their teens when Mickey retired. It was such a moment. You could feel it. The air was charged with a spontaneous outpouring of love and respect for the greatest woman golfer in the world. You don't plan to be a legend. You just become one.

*S*tick it high in the sky, strike the ball, and let it fly! When she's hot, she plays like AMY!! Juli Inkster is a three time U.S. amateur champion and has a daughter named Hayley. Life in orbit.

*S*he can go: miss cut, miss cut, win, win, win. All that and nice, too!

Donna White giving me the super raspberry.

Marlene Hagge –you warm my heart.

Lori West had her best money year in '92 and qualified for the Nabisco Dinah Shore. After years of struggle, it's good to see her have some success.

Beth. For four years I watched her hit shots that raised the hair on my arm involuntarily. Ten years flying fighters never did that.

*T*alk to it, Dale Eggeling.

*K*atherine Murphy, a photographer, snoozing in the Palm Springs desert sun.

*A*ngie Ridgeway with a bead on a birdie.

*B*etsy King in her "I've got it under control" set-up.

*L*PGA officials Barbara Trammell, Sandi Higgs, Beth McCombs and Mike Waldron staying dry at the very wet '92 U.S. Women's Open in Oakmont.

*I*ntense Dottie. Definitely in charge.

*S*usie Redman is a recent tour mother. Juggling babies and birdies. '92 was a very good year–she has talent.

*V*eteran tour caddies like Jeremiah fit in the "real caddy" elite status. Breakfast is a half inch of Crest, a Winston and two Buds. They go everywhere, they do their job well, and they add color to a somewhat mundane existence. The tour will suffer when they're gone.

*T*ara Fleming. How can anyone forget that smile?

*S*helley Hamlin at rest.

*L*ike all caddies, Ralph Scarinzi and John Dormann do things (A) for the money (B) 'cause they like golf (C) for the money (D) 'cause they have grass between their toes (E) all the above, but only a handful make any money.

*E*ternal optimism flows. Today is good – next week will be better, and next year will definitely be the best – with a few putts!

113

The seventh hole at Wykagyl is the longest par 3 on tour. It's approximately 215 yards to the center of the green. It's also a fan gathering spot. Getting to the northeast courses is a hassle, but when you finally get there, it's worth the effort.

Kris Tschetter at idle during the Sara Lee Classic.

Longtime caddy Larry Smich came on tour in the late '70s, and in spite of back problems, "Chronic Caddy Curse," he keeps going. The longer you stay out, the longer the grass gets between the toe

114

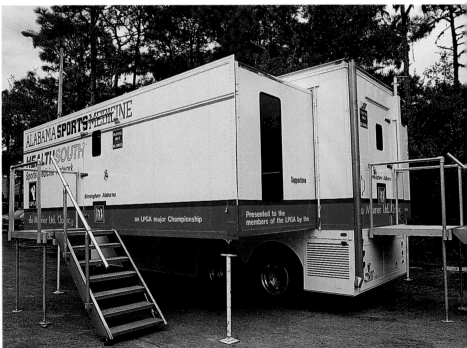

*T*he fitness van was a most welcome addition to the tour. With joint sponsorship by du Maurier Ltd., HealthSouth, Alabama Sports Medicine, American Sports Medicine Institute, and Ryder Systems, it is available at all U.S. tour sites. Player participation is over 80 percent.

115

*C*athy Mockett-Villa and her caddy, Richard Towne, looking over the situation.

*C*hris Johnson draws a bead on a putt at the McDonald's. Five of her six wins were on the western courses.

*J*oe DiMaggio was in Nancy's pro am group at the Nabisco Dinah Shore. Nancy's caddy, Tommy Thorpe, was dying to get a shot with DiMaggio. Joe was most cooperative, as you can see.

*J*ill Briles-Hinton and Tammie Green working hard for those tourney bucks. If it were easy, they'd call it bowling.

Debbie Raso told me that Hollis Stacy's caddy, Bebe, was in a hospital in Florida with lung cancer. I called that night. "Hello Bebe, it's Dee. What the hell you doing in the hospital"? "Hey Dee, I'm fine. I'll be back out soon." We chatted some. Bebe didn't make it. I think about him a lot.

This photo of Kristi Albers is my favorite golf action shot. Her balance is so good. Everything is just perfect.

"Putter Bob" pushing his putter cards at the McDonald's event.

*M*arshals at the ninth tee waiting for the first group during the Mixed Team.

*B*etsy Barrett generating a blast of sand and grass at the sorely missed Orange Blossom Classic in St. Petersburg, Florida.

The Nabisco Dinah Shore brings out the best in everybody. Fans, players, marshals, and photographers – lots of photographers. BIG EVENT.

Martha Nause showing some style.

A tip of the cap to you too, Nancy Harvey.

Terry Galvin, editor of Golf World Magazine, *was in Tallahassee, covering the '93 Sprint Classic. He was admiring Mickey Wright's ancient set of Wilson sticks. After watching her bold putts, we agreed— legends don't lag!*

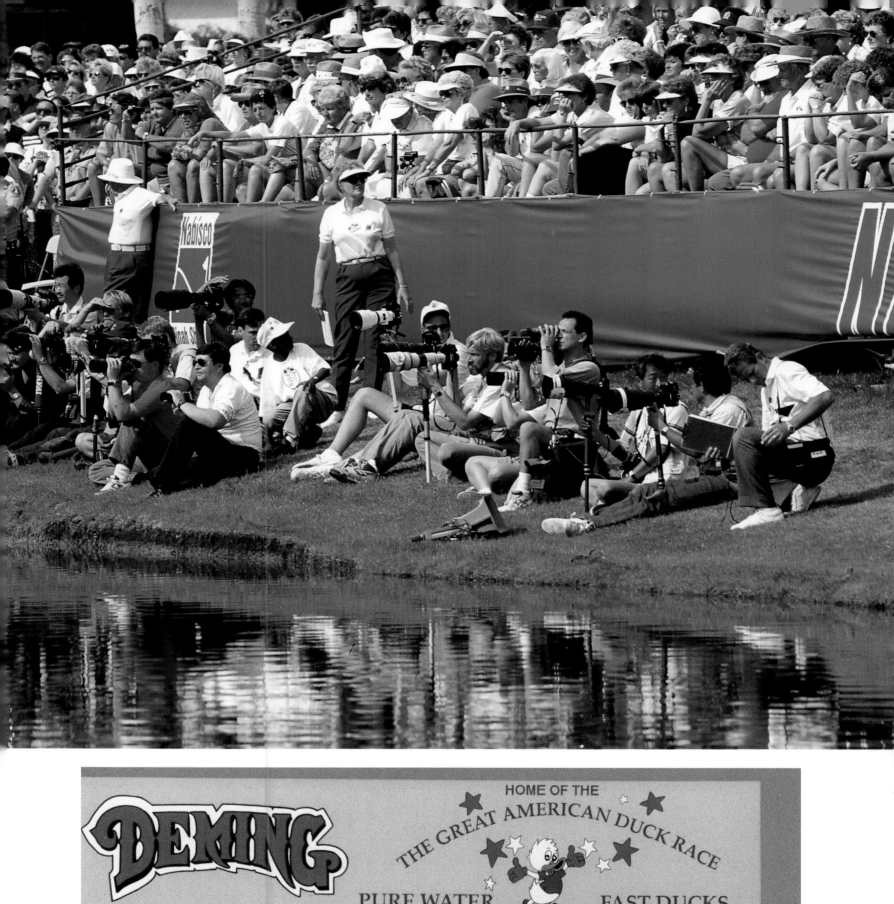

*E*very year the tour leaves Florida via I-10 to Tucson. A meal at Petros Truck stop in El Paso makes crossing Texas bearable. The next pulse-racing event is Deming, New Mexico. I can't wait to see that big road sign "Pure water – fast Ducks." Three hundred days a year on the road! Being simple minded helps.

Maggie Will's first pro win in Vegas in 1990. She's a mudder – both of her wins were under very tough weather conditions.

DESERT INN
LPGA INTERNATIONAL
March 7-11,1990

March 11, 1990

Pay to the
Order of MAGGIE WILL /$60,000⁰⁰

SIXTY THOUSAND DOLLARS and ⁿ⁰/₁₀₀

Cathy Morse – the photo says it all!

Judi Pavon – the tours only lefty since Bonnie Bryant retired.

Classic Amy Alcott. Needs one more win for Hall of Fame. I don't know any one who isn't pulling for her.

*W*e were all down at the Nestle World Championship at Lake Lanier, Georgia, in 1990. BIG TOURNAMENT– LOTS OF BUCKS– PRESSURE!
Jane Geddes and Patty Rizzo were riding my wife's wave runner –
check the eyes on Jane, lower left, just before she slam dunks Rizzo.
So much for pressure. Personally, I prefer the men's tour
where it's all serious and Daddy Warbucks – NOT!

*H*ollis Stacy has a routine: sight, take it back, step into the shot. I've tried for a hundred rolls to capture the movement–Gotcha Hollis!

Hollis likes me cause I have a lens she wants.
Won't smile unless you're handsome!

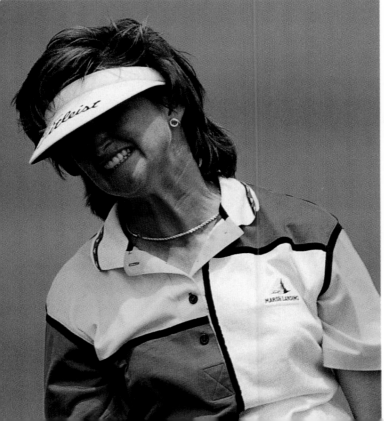

I was locked on Deb Richard hitting a fairway to green shot.
It wasn't until I got the film back that I saw her
"I hate this game" expression. She's a
good player and a quality person.

127

*"**C**ome on, Dee, take a family photo!" So Ray, Nancy, Ashley, Erinn, Torri and their nanny, Holly, lined up for this shot.*

*S*ometimes when Ray's schedule permits and the tournaments are close, he'll bring the girls and they'll follow Mom on an early morning practice round. How many super stars can handle that?

*R*ay caddied for me at the Nabisco in 1989 when I was injured. They're talking yardage here on No. 17 tee.

*T*his is one of my favorite shots – Ray and Domingo – Nancy's father, walking in cadence during a practice round at the 1992 U. S. Women's Open.

129

*D*ana Lofland and her husband, John Dormann, who caddies for Meg Mallon, were in Las Vegas. Golf World Magazine *was doing a special on them, and I took the photos.*

*K*athy Guadagnino is one of 12 LPGA members to make the Women's Open her first victory. Would you have guessed that many?

*I*nkster with her birdie blade. She won't do that in a thunderstorm. Too hot!

One of the tour's nicest people is a caddy named Jeff Cable–"Tree" to his friends. I was goofing off at the mixed team when a lady came by and asked if I ever took pictures of caddy's moms. I told her to taxi right back up there on the tee, and I'd see if my camera works. Nice family. Mom, Shirley, and sister Debbie.

Melissa McNamara is so warm and friendly. She can say "Good Morning" and make my whole day.

Photography–hours of boredom sprinkled with magic moments. This is just one piece of massive equipment needed to telecast a golf event.

131

*S*herri Turner is about five foot nothing and really slams the ball. She played great in '88. Her caddy here is my wife, Jeannie. This shot was taken at the JCPenney Classic in Bardmoor, Florida.

*Sherri is a diabetic and has a constant fight going to maintain competitive status.
She has won three times in spite of this handicap.*

133

*D*ana Lofland's exciting putt on the 18th green Sunday in Las Vegas clinched her first professional win in April '92. She led all four days to win her second title at the McCall's Classic at Stratton Mountain, Vt., in '93.

*B*arb Mucha keeps getting better.
Her two wins could multiply.

*J*oan Joyce, one of softball's all time elite,
still plays a pretty good golf game.

*I*f you could bottle the body language and facial expression of
Kris Monaghan as the ball slides by the hole, it would be priceless.

If Caroline Keggi got any lower, she'd be looking up at the ball. I couldn't do that when I was ten.

*J*oan Pitcock. I've known her since she was about 13.
Her mom would bring her to the San Jose Classic, and she would follow
Beth Daniel and me around the golf course. I took her through pro school
at Sweetwater, Texas, in 1987 when she got her playing card.

*P*am Wright – friendly little furriner! Hails from Scotland and was on the '92
winning Solheim Cup team.

*J*ane Geddes would work with Derek Hardy at Snee Farm Country Club in the late '70's.
I was a member there and would watch her practice.

Her fans made the Hall Calls sign on speculation – her player friends had the champagne ready in anticipation, and Patty reflects the solemn moment as she holds the winning trophy that put her in the Hall of Fame. I'm the lucky guy who watched it all and caught a few of the moments before they faded away. Maybe down the line, I'll be near another lucky spot.

140

*O*nce you reach a certain proficiency with a camera, luck plays a large part in capturing an event on film. Being near the lucky spot is, of course, essential.Watching Patty's superb play Saturday at the Standard Register Ping Classic in March '93 alerted me to her win potential.

This simple, straight forward photo captures Donna White's warmth and personality. A real person in a sometimes unreal profession.

Pat Bradley plays well with anyone on her bag. She plays much better with Jerry "Woody" Woodard, however. They have been together 10 years and have won 21 tournaments.

Beth Daniel and Greg Sheridan enjoying the hug of victory at the 1990 Centel Classic in Tallahassee.

The 1993 President of the Ladies Professional Golf Association, Miss Alice Miller! Good Luck to you, good friend.

143

She is Deborah McHaffie, not Debbie.
She is specific about that. I thought you might
like to know. She is fun to photograph and her work
ethic is starting to produce results.

*J*ane Crafter won the Australian Masters in December '92.

*T*he two Cindy's (Schreyer and Figg-Currier) earned their way into the Nabisco Dinah Shore with top three finishes.

*M*aggie Will just won her first professional tournament, and her caddy, Bob Kendall, is showing his appreciation.

*P*atty Berg Presents the "Patty Berg" Award to Judy Dickinson for 1992.

*I*n December 1992 the LPGA held a social function at Innisbrook Country Club during the annual Mixed Team event. The purpose was to raise funds for the LPGA Foundation, a non-profit charitable organization, and to honor Judy Dickinson for her precedent-setting three-year tenure as President of the LPGA.

*T*wo well established and popular Hall of Famers: Patty Berg and Kathy Whitworth.

*L*PGA incoming president Alice Miller and outgoing president Judy Dickinson.

*J*udy and Gardner Dickinson's twin boys, Barron and Spencer, seen earlier as toddlers. They're growing fast.

I like tight action shots like this of Laura Davies. It lets you sneak inside the visor and get in on the action.

*A*lice Ritzman just keeps getting better. She came on tour in 1978. I know she's happy cause it shows.

*J*ane Geddes doing her "get out of my face, Dee" routine.

*P*hotos like this one of Joan Pitcock really make me appreciate the Minolta metering system. The third tee at Bethesda has some interesting back lighting.

149

During the mid '80s the most popular tour stop for everybody was the Sleepy Hole G.C. in Portsmouth, Virginia.
Some of us started a caddy/player-chicken-and-beer softball party on Wednesday of tourney week. It grew into a 300-people-plus event.
Nancy squiggled one down first baseline and got thrown out.

*N*ancy and her long-time caddy Roscoe were clowning around at the party. Roscoe passed away in 1989. He was a tour caddy original. Nancy loved him dearly.

*B*roadcaster, Kathleen Sullivan, is an active ProAm participant and a strong supporter of the LPGA.

*V*al Skinner and I teamed up in 1986 and won the very first event, the Mazda Classic at Stonebridge. She's a power player and a very talented person. I enjoyed working for her.

*W*ho could it be under the Sara Lee??

A rather intense Caroline Keggi – a tour sleeper!

*B*randie Burton and John Schiffer on the 17th green at the Dinah. Memorize the name Brandie. She's just 21. I couldn't answer the phone at that age!

153

*B*randie Burton hit a beautiful draw around the corner on No. 9 at the Dinah.
In the early '80s you could fly the corner 'cause the trees were small – not now!

*P*atty Sheehan and Jody Anschutz were discussing world affairs, and Jody's caddy, Lane, was interpreting.

154

Liselotte Neumann on 18th tee at McDonalds.

Rosie Jones doing her thing at Inverrary.

I caught Rhonda Glenn airing her views on the eighth hole at the '92 Dinah. Her book "Illustrated History of Women's Golf" was recently released.

*N*ancy Harvey and hubby Glen during a lull in play at the 18th tee in Delaware.

*T*he first ever senior tourney for LPGA players over 50. Centel sponsored the event in 1991 at Tallahassee. Sandra Palmer beat Kathy Whitworth in the 36-hole, 12 player tournament.

Shirley Englehorn
Sandra Spuzich
Marilynn Smith
Betsy Rawls
Kathy Whitworth
Carol Mann
Louise Suggs
Murle Breer
Clifford Ann Creed
Marlene Hagge
Jo Ann Prentice
Sandra Palmer

*"I'll teach you to give me bad yardage"! Carner and "Red" Hartkop on the range in Phoenix.
She didn't hurt Red, but she ruined her five iron.*

*T*ammie Green awaiting her tee time at the 1990 U.S. Women's Open in Atlanta.

*J*ane Blalock: The best course manager I ever saw.

A lady was walking past me at the 18th tee at McDonald's— she had something on her back under a yellow slicker. I called her and asked if I could take a shot – check that pacifier sticking out under Donald's eyes!

*J*ohn Foust, Nina's dad, used to caddy for Nina several times a year. Now that he's retired I see him out looping it everywhere. What is it about retired folks? Don't they ever retire?

*P*atty Sheehan and caddy, Carl Laib, the "Caddy Machine", during a practice round at the '92 U.S. Women's Open in Oakmont.

*S*ometimes simple things can fill a page – flying grass and the graceful swing of Nancy Scranton.

*D*ottie's anguish on a near make putt. She works hard and takes the game seriously.

*K*ris Tschetter's fun on the driving range,
and a birdie line up by Michelle Mackall.
Nice memories!

161

*J*ohn Manfredi, Dottie Mochrie, Mark Rolfing and Dinah Shore enjoying the victory festivities. What could be finah than to win the Dinah? Dottie won a hard battle with Juli Inkster in '92. It's one of the four majors, but it's just a "little" more than that.

*C*athy Gerring has her career on hold while recovering from severe burns on her face and hands in 1992. The tour and fans wish her a speedy recovery.

A sign of the times. The bottom of McHaffie's golf bag.

*P*ostie makes a good living but earns every dime. She's a true workhorse and a solid rock in the profession.

*S*hirley Furlong and her caddy, Carla Harper, taking time out for a quick flick.

Meg Mallon beating balls in Phoenix. Practice makes perfect...sometimes.

My hip was killing me at the first Solheim Cup at Lake Nona in Orlando in 1990. I couldn't fight the crowd so I backed off on a knoll with the long lens and caught Kathy Whitworth accepting the winning trophy from Karsten Solheim.

Juli Inkster firing off into space at the '92 Mazda. It wasn't her best day, but she'll make up for it.

Marta Figueras-Dotti is Spain's first professional female golfer. She's come close several times. I would like to see her win.

Bring some binoculars sometime and watch Kate Hughes set up. Her intensity is something to see. What a fireball!

Beth's ball was snuggled down in long grass. She and Greg were trying to figure what it would do. It spit out like Tabasco mouthwash.

Dottie and Sammy Sigh are so special. As master calligraphers they do wonders for tournament score boards. Please don't retire.

Florence Descampe. She won her rookie year and was on the winning European Solheim Cup team, both in '92.

*F*orgive me, Kathryn Young, but it's such a good shot. Good golf is never good enough and bad golf is the end of the world.

Laurie Rinker-Graham and I became friends back in '87 when I carried her bag. She's a two-time collegiate All-American from the University of Florida.

Michelle Estill won the Ping-Cellular One event in '91, her first full year on tour. Pretty good!

Vicki Goetz made the cut in '93 at Crooked Stick, her first U.S. Women's Open as a professional. With her short game and good attitude, she should do well.

*P*atty Sheehan and John Killeen worked together for a number of years and had much success. This shot on the ninth green in San Diego is one of my favorites. It has it all: the ball-the player-the caddy-the flag stick-the logo. Too bad Patty missed the putt. John looks like a Stealth Bomber in take-off position.

The weather Sunday at the '92 LPGA Championship was nasty; rainy, cloudy, low-vis duck paradise. I was pushing Fuji film to the limit when Alfredsson made a half acre putt on No. 4.

*C*heck that birdie stride! Helen is a lively bold-faced slugger with many wins and much ado in her future. Her first American victory was the Nabisco Dinah Shore in Palm Springs in 1993.

Laura Davies and her brother, Tony, waiting their turn at McDonald's sixth hole. Tony gave up his position "Inside the Ropes" in '93 and is Laura's new business manager. You're gonna miss it, Tony!

Most professional photographers wouldn't give you sand in the desert. These guys are no exception. When they get too cocky, I remind them that I had nearly 200 combat missions in the Photo Phantom (RF4C) before they graduated from school. Michael Cohen shoots for Golf For Women Magazine, *Bob Strauss and Steve Wilson both freelance. They're good friends. With their help I've gone from minimum magnificent to maximum mediocre.*

Jay Randolph and Mary Bryan doing a promo at the Mazda Championship. The LPGA is making headway in every venture .

Jerry Potter's by-line is prominent in USA Today. *He covers golf in general and the LPGA in particular. I like him 'cause he laughs at my jokes.*

173

*J*ohn Killeen, who caddies for Okamoto, and Nancy Lopez were wishing me a happy birthday. It occurs during McDonald's week most years. It's fun to be remembered.

*N*ancy Ramsbottom was planning her route to the green from her stray second shot at the '93 Mazda. She made par.

*M*issie Berteotti is rapidly becoming the best player not to have a win. Her play in the '90s is very strong. Any time now! Zounds!! Dee the Prophet—UPDATE! Missie just won the Ping/Welch's Championship in August '93.

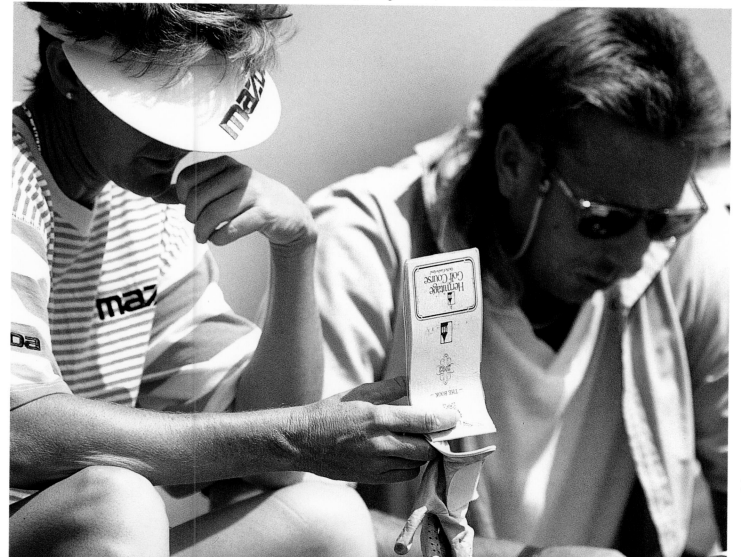

*B*eth and Caddy, Greg Sheridan, looking at notes in their yardage books at the Sara Lee Classic.

175

*C*indy Mackey won her first tournament at the Master Card in Westchester County, N.Y. in 1986

*L*ori Garbacz was resting when I came up behind her. She heard me and gave me this great smile.

*B*etsy King on the practice tee. Good ole Betsy. She's probably thinking, "I'm gonna bust you right in the face, Whitey."

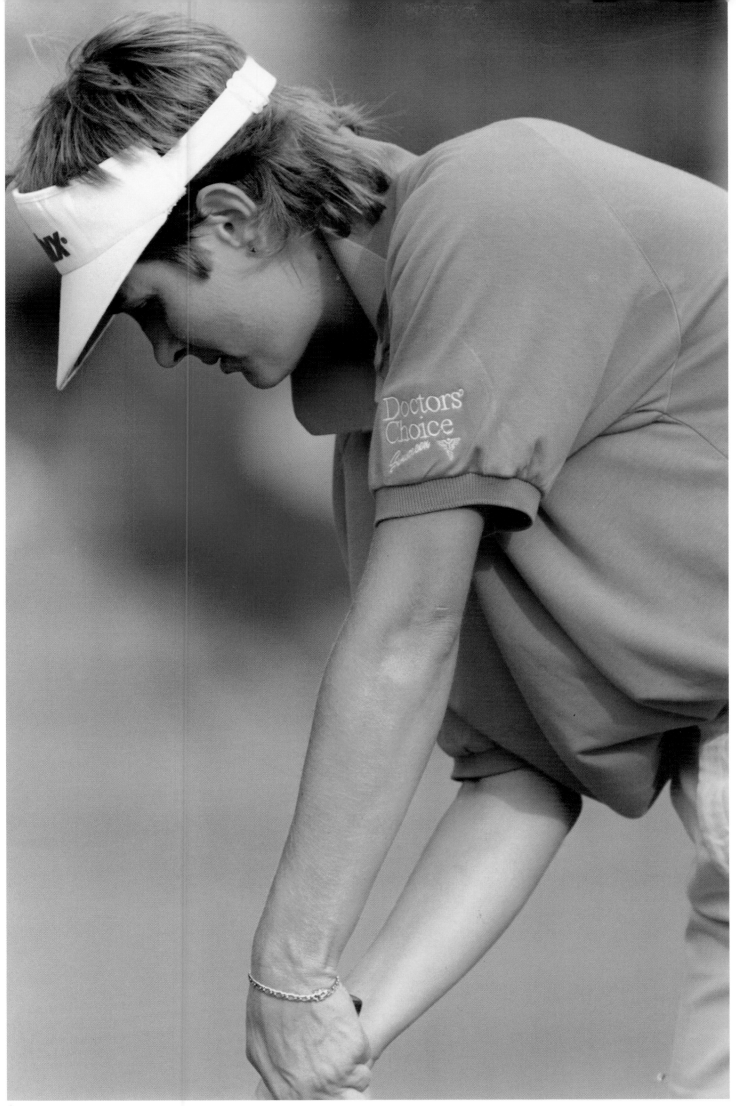

I like this shot of Muffin. Her putting stance is as unique as she is herself. I kid her about being on loan from the Martian Tour.

Sandra Spuzich and Joyce Kazmierski. Spuz and Kaz. I greet them as "Hi, favorite people" – that's how I feel.

178

Heather Drew and Allison Finney giving me the waves during a practice round at the Dinah. They're the only people I know friendlier than me.

*B*lond hair flying, bouncy and energetic. On the leader board. Must be Cindy Rarick.

The Mechem family, Marilyn, Charlie and Allison were out on No. 11 at the Nabisco Dinah Shore during ProAm day. I didn't think I had enough light, but the shot came out just fine.

It's hard to take a bad shot of Sally Little. This is a true snap shot of her at the Mixed Team JCPenney Classic in 1986,

*M*ochrie placing the ball in perfect putting position.

*M*allon family affair in Oakmont at the '92 U.S. Women's Open. Her mom, Marian, and dad, John.

*M*elissa McNamara: A fresh breeze.

*R*osie Jones nailing a nugget. She had nine top-10 finishes in '92.

*K*im Bauer looking for the press room.

1993 might be the year of Europe. Trish Johnson has won back to back in Las Vegas and Atlanta. She was also a member of the winning European Solheim Cup. This lady can play.

The fifth hole at the Dinah is a picturesque par 3. It's beautiful early in the morning with the sunlight bouncing off the water onto the distant mountains. Meg Mallon and caddy, John Dormann, are studying the yardage. Hit the six, Meg!

We were flying back from the Jamaica Classic in 1988. Lori Garbacz was seated ahead of me. Seems I always catch her looking back. With shots like this, maybe I'll keep it up.

The Mazda Championship initiated a telephone call-in question and answer session a while back that has become quite popular with D.C. area golfers. Patty Berg, Marlene Hagge, and Kathy Whitworth were donating their time and sharing their knowledge of the game with the fans in '93.

184

Clea Artis Wiley and Alice Miller have been a caddy/player team for some years now. Wiley drives the fitness van and tractor to each tournament site. He's a good caddy and a good friend.

Jill Briles-Hinton – "The Accordion." How does she do that?

Steve Ellis is editor of Golf Week, the Orlando based publication. It"s a fast growing editorial, facts and stats for true golf fans. Steve is a long time fan of the LPGA.

Beth Daniel and Golf World Magazine features editor, Geoff Russell, had a bet on the Masters. Beth Won!

Stephanie Maynor getting set to tee off.

In a former life Deborah McHaffie was a magnet. She draws fans including one retired old geezer photographer.

*O*n Sunday of the '92 Mazda LPGA Championship, Juli Inkster and her caddy Ralph Scarinzi teed off tied for second place. A series of events, mostly a stray driver, knocked them down to ninth place and out of the big money. This photo captures the care, concern, and respect that tour caddies have for their players. "You gave it your best, Pro. Go home, relax, forget it. See you Tuesday in Corning."

*C*aroline Pierce is a friendly transplant from Sussex, England. She is having a nice career, and I wish her well.

Please
DO NOT ASK
FOR AUTOGRAPHS
DURING PLAY

*S*ometimes the players will allow their caddies a few moments to practice being people. That's enough, Donna and John! Back to caddy status.

*D*ottie Mochrie and Dan Forsman accepting the winning check at the JCPenney Classic in Tarpon Springs, Florida, in '92. That's a $110,000 smile on Dottie.

*B*etsy King's relaxed mood at the Nabisco Dinah Shore. She was giving an open-air interview.

189

*F*ormer tour player Marlene Floyd offering live color commentary.

I was an old established caddy when Patty Sheehan was a rookie. We met on the sixth hole of Deer Creek C.C. in Florida during a practice round in 1981. I was convinced then that she would be a great player, and, obviously, time has proven me a sage.

Patty has the obvious traits like charm and talent, but there is so much more. She's very funny. She laughs and clowns around a lot. She loves golf, but I feel it's the means not the end of life for her. I like Pitty Pat. Have from day one.

*T*he front of the 13th green at Innisbrook is steep and many golf balls go in the water. These two marshals were performing a co-operative acrobatic maneuver to recover a prized golf ball. Nice work, fellows!

*T*he putter, and the stroke that made Nancy rich, put her in the Hall of Fame, and along with her smile, made her one of the most popular players to ever put on spikes. And folks – she's not through yet.

*D*on and JoAnne Carner will probably stay on tour forever. When they're not playing golf, they're fishing. What's to retire?

*B*eth was getting a frosted "Do" in San Jose when she decided to get some fresh air. Bad timing, Beth!

*J*oAnne Carner all laid out on the fairway in Phoenix. A bad back is walking misery.

*L*ynn Connelly was voted onto the player council for 1994. She is a good player and active member of the LPGA.

*P*atty Sheehan's pert, pink personality.

*F*ans of the JAL Big Apple Classic at Wykagyl will remember this scene during tournament week.

*K*im Bauer figuring an eight-way break at Wykagyl.

*T*his fine gentleman was a marshal on No. 8 at the Mixed Team.
He was working on his swing

Amy Benz's caddy, Donna Earley, tending the flag at the Nabisco Dinah Shore in '92.

Tani Tatum. Just the friendliest person you'll ever meet.

Elaine Crosby: Very steady – constant improvement.

Jan Stephenson was an established player with one win when I came on tour in 1976. I think history will show that she has done as much as anyone to promote and advance the image of the LPGA as a quality, professional group. She has won three of the four modern "Major" events. Pat Bradley is the only player to beat that.

*B*etsy King and her caddy, Gary Harrison, conversing during a lull in play at the LPGA Championship in '92.

*N*ina Foust getting better all the time – I would love to see her win.

I was shooting on the 18th tee at the McDonald's tourney in Delaware in a warm, light rain. A fan behind me was sitting on the grass under a tree, oblivious to golf, rain, crowds and camera, sound asleep.

199

*F*rom sand blasting Gail Graham to Carolyn Hill to wise-acre Joan Pitcock or long-time caddy buddy Rick Aune. Turn a corner most any day and you'll run into Colleen Walker or an old friend like Carol Mann, a 38-tournament-win Hall of Famer. The LPGA Tour – easy flowing friendships everywhere.

*C*arol Mann

*C*arolyn Hill

*J*oan Pitcock

*C*olleen Walker

*R*ick Aune

*C*harlie Mechem is a hands-on, active commissioner. Shown here with Suzanne Jackson and Nabisco Tournament Director, Mike Galeski, his enthusiasm burns brightly in everything he does. This little tour of mine — I'm gonna make it shine!

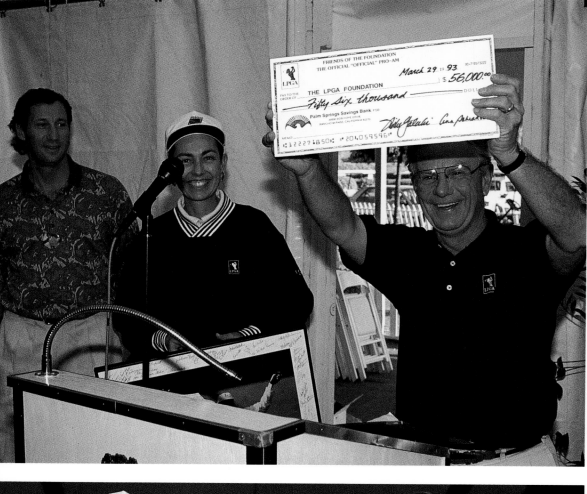

*S*uzanne Jackson, Jackie Bertsch and Beth Daniel at the '93 Suzanne Jackson Benefit Pro/Am on Monday following the Nabisco Dinah Shore. Jackie and Mike Galeski, the Nabisco Tournament Director, conceived and organized the Pro/Am on a completely voluntary, cost free basis. Nabisco provided the golf course and facilities, Mazda provided the food and beverages, all prizes were donated and Pro/Am participants volunteered their time. Over 56,000 dollars was raised for the LPGA Foundation. Caring and sharing — a big part of the LPGA.

*B*etsy blasting sand on No. 11 at San Diego in 1990. When she doesn't win, sometimes I feel like asking her if she's resting or just tired of paying taxes.

Inkster under the 'brella. She won two major tourneys her rookie year. Sneaks up on everybody and stabs them with her putter - a true lightning bolt.

Lauri Merten and her fiancé, Louis Capano Jr., were hovering in a happy high following Lauri's sudden victory in the '93 U.S. Women's Open. She birdied Nos. 16 and 18 to beat Helen Alfredsson by a stroke. Miracle maker Merten, My! My!

Ayako Okamoto is getting Americanized. She's starting to show some emotions out on the links. She is Japan's media event. Great player.

Bill Spencer, who conceived and designed the book, and I hope you enjoyed your visit "Inside the Ropes." We started with Beth teeing it up, and we end with the hand-off of the putter on 18.

End may not be the appropriate word. I hope this is the beginning. There is always a first tee. If you have enjoyed our book, come out to a tour site and see for yourself. The players are real and fresh and talented. You will become a fan. I'm living proof.

INDEX